Bettendorf Public Library
Information Center
www.bettendorflibrary.com

VIOLIN SOLOS ON BRAZILIAN THEMES

MB99565

BY FLAVIO HENRIQUE MEDEIROS, CARLOS ALMADA AND THIAGO LYRA

FREE PIANO ACCOMPANIMENT AVAILABLE ONLINE! VISIT: WWW.MELBAY.COM/99565

This book was provided for

by

Raising money to support, enhance and preserve Bettendorf Public Library programs and services.

© 2010 BY MEL BAY PUBLICATIONS, INC., PACIFIC, MO 63069.
ALL RIGHTS RESERVED. INTERNATIONAL COPYRIGHT SECURED. B.M.I. MADE AND PRINTED IN U.S.A
No part of this publication may be reproduced in whole or in part, or stored in a retrieval system, or transmitted in any form or by any means, electronic, mechanical, photocopy, recording, or otherwise, without written permission of the publisher.

Visit us on the Web at www.melbay.com or www.billsmusicshelf.com

Introduction

Brazil offers a great and luxurious musical variety, not only for its large extension of land, but also for the multiple cultural interchange established along centuries among the several peoples which contributed to the forming of its rich and varied musical map.

From that triple (though not always conscious) alliance among the native Indigenous, the European colonizer and the African (those latter brought here as slave workers), resulted a "Brazility" feeling which is common to every country side, despite the distances that separate them: joyous, melancholic, nostalgic or ritual, Brazilian music is always the most authentic expression of its people, their hapiness and sorrows.

This work is an effort to display some Brazilian popular folk melodies arranged for violin and piano. The themes chosen, coming from the country as well as urban areas, are part of a repertoire quite familiar to every Brazilian, some of them already belonging for centuries to Brazil's memory. No intention of producing a scientific or musicological work has been nourished by the arrangers. What guided them in the choice of the songs presented in this book was, above all, a poetic sense and deep love for the music of their country

Carlos Almada, Flavio Henrique Medeiros & Thiago Lyra

TABLE OF CONTENTS

Introduction	1
A canoa virou	4
Balaio	5
Beira-mar	6
Coco do Engenho Novo	8
Estácio	10
Faz hoje um ano	12
Jabirá	13
Muié rendeira	14
O cravo brigou com a rosa	16
Ó mana, deixa eu ir!	18
Os peixinhos do mar	19
Peixe vivo	20
Prenda minha	21
Romance sertanejo	22
Sereno	24
Terço	26
Terezinha de Jesus	27
Truléu	28
Vinde, vinde, moços e velhos / Pai Francisco	30

A canoa virou

VIOLIN

Arranged by Carlos Almada

Balaio

VIOLIN Arranged by Carlos Almada

Beira-Mar

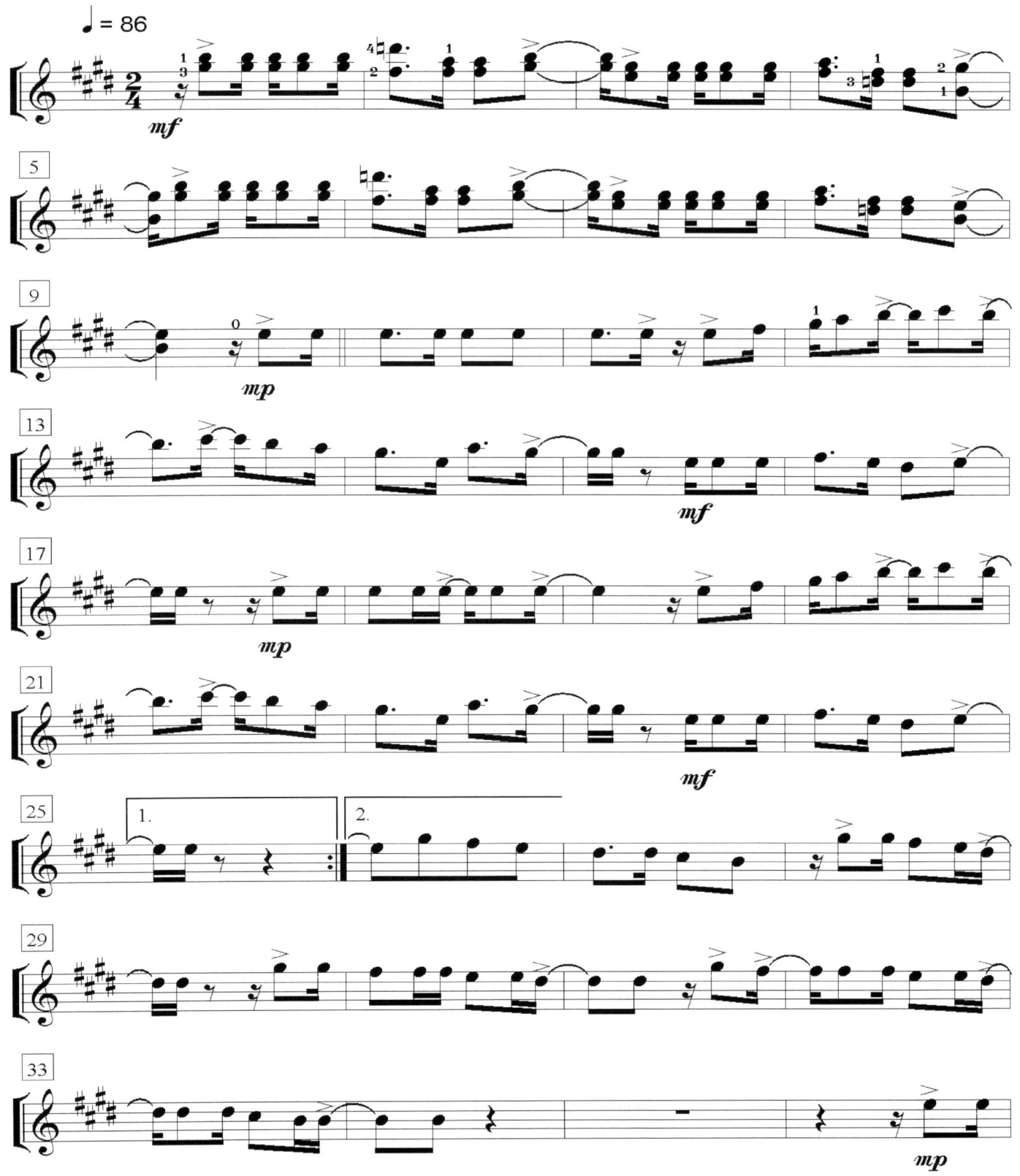

Coco do Engenho Novo

arranged by Flavio Henrique Medeiros

VIOLIN

This page has been left blank
to avoid awkward page turns.

Estácio, Mangueira

Faz hoje um ano

VIOLIN

Arranged by Thiago Lyra

Jabirá

VIOLIN

Arranged by Thiago Lyra

Muié rendeira

This page has been left blank
to avoid awkward page turns.

O cravo brigou com a rosa

Arranged by Thiago Lyra

VIOLIN

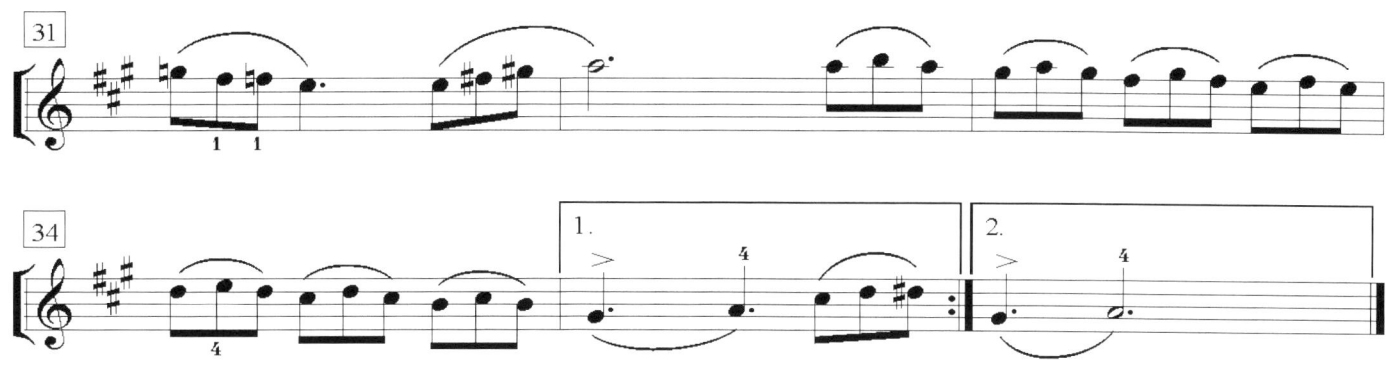

Ó mana, deixa eu ir!

Arranged by Thiago Lyra

VIOLIN

Os peixinhos do mar

VIOLIN

Arranged by Carlos Almada

Peixe vivo

VIOLIN

Arranged by Carlos Almada

Prenda minha

VIOLIN

Arranged by Carlos Almada

Romance Sertanejo

VIOLIN

Arranged by Flavio Henrique Medeiros

This page has been left blank
to avoid awkward page turns.

Sereno

VIOLIN

Arranged by Flavio Henrique Medeiros

24

Terço

Terezinha de Jesus

VIOLIN
Arranged by Carlos Almada

Truléu, Léu, Léu, Léu, Léu

Arranged by Flavio Henrique Medeiros

This page has been left blank
to avoid awkward page turns.

Vinde, Vinde, Moços e Velhos / Pai Francisco

Arranged by Flavio Henrique Medeiros

VIOLIN

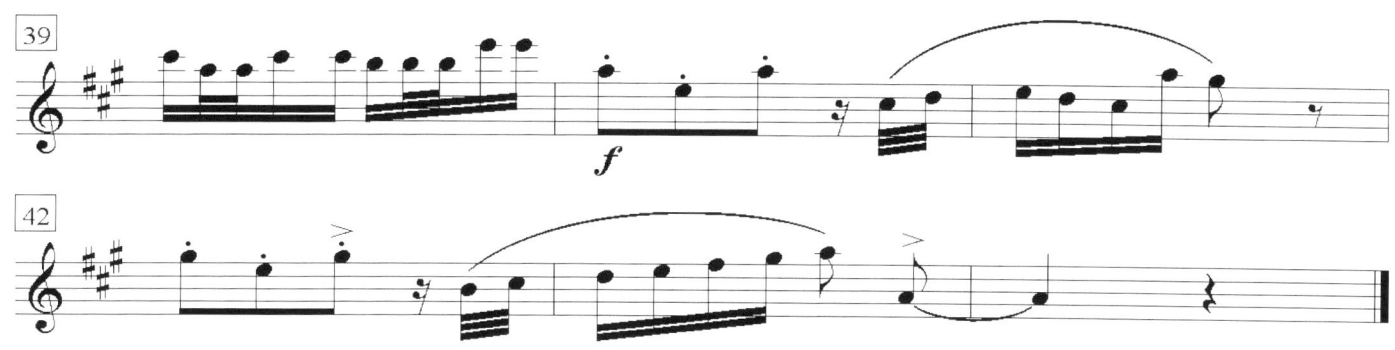

UNIQUELY INTERESTING MUSIC!

Made in the USA
Charleston, SC
16 January 2011